CW00686746

# REVENGE

# REVENGE
## A Thriller
## by Robin Hawdon

Warner Chappell Plays

LONDON

A Time Warner Company

First published 1991
by Warner Chappell Plays Ltd.,
129 Park Street, London W1Y 3FA

Copyright © 1991 by Robin Hawdon

ISBN 0 85676 143 5

Printed by Commercial Colour Press, London E7

REVENGE was first presented by Redgrave Theatre
Productions in association with Mark Furness Ltd at the
Redgrave Theatre, Farnham, on 23 January, 1991, with the
following cast:

BILL CRAYSHAW, MP    Simon Ward
MARY STANWYCK        Fiona Fullerton

Directed by Graham Watkins
Designed by Sally Howard
Lighting designed by Mark Doubleday

The action takes place within the Westminster apartment of
Bill Crayshaw, MP in the present

## ACT ONE

Evening

## ACT TWO

A few seconds later

## ACT ONE

*The setting is the London penthouse apartment of Bill Crayshaw, MP, near Westminster. Ultra-modern, ultra-stylish, ultra-impressive — the urban domain of a wealthy man. Huge picture window overlooking the city, valuable paintings, sculptures and objets d'art. Book-shelves filled with first editions and leather-bound volumes. A drinks cabinet. A shelf of photographs.*

*One corner of the room is equipped as a 'hi-tec' office area. Modern desk, filing cabinets, fax machine, shredding machine, TV monitor, mobile telephone.*

*Upstage a wide opening to a lobby area off which is the rest of the apartment, and at the rear of which is a front door to the passage. When this is open a lift can be seen beyond it. The only other door visible is on one side down-stage which leads to some service stairs.*

*Evening. The apartment is empty. It is lit from the glow of London through the big picture window. There is the sound of a lift ascending from outside the apartment. A key rattles in the lock and* BILL CRAYSHAW *enters, switching on the lights. He is around forty, confident, charming, tough as nails. He wears an expensive coat and carries an overnight case.*

*He puts the case down, takes off his coat, and flings it over a chair in the lobby, then takes some papers from a side pocket in the case. He enters the main room, goes to the drinks cabinet and pours himself a large vodka and tonic. Goes to the fax machine and studies one or two messages that have come in. Switches on the television screen and, using the remote control scrolls through the current share-price listings. He collapses in a chair with a sigh of relief, and takes a long pull at his drink while comparing the prices to a list on the papers he is holding, then picks up a mobile telephone and taps out a number.*

BILL          Geoffrey? It's me. I've just got in from the airport. How's it going? I see our price is up another 6p. What's the latest on the Cargill Trust side? (*He looks at one of the fax messages.*) Yes, I've got a fax on that. How is the old boy reacting? We're getting there, Geoffrey,

but we need that final commitment from
New York. Will you know tonight? Good —
call me as soon as you do. Either here or at
Susie's. (*Smiles*.) You can interrupt anything
for that.

(*He taps another number*.)

Susie, angel, how are you? I've just got back
from Frankfurt. Of course ... I've just got
one or two things to see to — such as say
hello to my wife — then I'll be over.

(*The house intercom phone buzzes. He glances at
it*.)

That's the house phone — I'll have to answer
it. (*Grins*.) Sounds wonderful. Keep it hot for
me.

(*As he switches off, the house phone buzzes again.
He answers it*.)

Yes, George? Who? Who is she? Well, who
does she say she is? I don't know — tell her I
can't see anyone, I'm too busy.

(BILL *replaces the receiver and goes to replenish
his glass. He is studying the share prices on the TV
again when the mobile phone rings. He answers
it*.)

Yes? Speaking. Police? What's the problem?
Mark Tilling — yes, he's my party agent.
(*Pause*.) Oh my God — when? How did it
happen? Is he ...? Oh God. Why did no
one inform me earlier? Yes, I've been in
Frankfurt for the last thirty-six hours, but I'm
always contactable. Who else knows?

(*The house phone rings again. He ignores it*.)

Yes, I see. I'll be at the House of Commons
tomorrow morning, and down at my
constituency office in the afternoon. I'll wait
to hear from you. Thank you.

(*Switches off and stands in thought for a moment. The house phone rings again, which he answers impatiently.*)

What now, George? Well if she won't say what she wants, how . . . .? What does that mean? And you've checked her over? The size of her bust is immaterial, George — is she bona fide? (*Pause.*) Oh hell — very well, send her up. But tell her I've got a crisis on and it's got to be quick. And no one else tonight, George — not even the PM on bended knee.

(*He replaces the receiver.*)

(*muttering*) That'll be the day.

(*Thinks for a moment, taps another number on the mobile phone.*)

Joanna? I'm back. You've heard about Mark? It happened yesterday morning, I must have been on the plane at the time. Christ, we were only having dinner with him the night before. The news hasn't broken yet — apparently they've only just managed to get official identification of the body. I can't Jo, I'm shattered — I've only just got back from the airport. I've got one or two things to see to, then I'm going straight to bed.

(*The lift is heard arriving.*)

There's a committee meeting at the House tomorrow, but I'll be down after that. Right.

(*He switches off the phone. The door buzzer goes.*)

Jesus Christ! (*Calling.*) Just a minute.

(*Looking around the room, he switches off the TV, puts the papers he has been studying into the shredding machine and switches it on, destroying them. He goes to the front door and opens it.*

> MARY *stands there. She is in her early thirties,*
> *attractive, with a slight regional accent, perhaps*
> *Scottish. She is fair-haired, and wears spectacles.*
> *She carries a handbag and a briefcase.*)

MARY    May I come in?

BILL    What do you want?

MARY    Just a few words.

BILL    You've come at a bad moment. Is it very
        urgent?

MARY    (*entering past him*) It won't take long, please.

BILL    Why can't you make an appointment like
        everyone else?

MARY    I didn't have time. (*She looks round.*) Some
        place. Not what I expected somehow.

BILL    What do you mean?

MARY    The style.

BILL    You don't like the style?

MARY    Oh very impressive. But more a bachelor's
        than a married man's.

BILL    Well I am more or less a bachelor in London.

MARY    Sorry?

BILL    My wife spends most of her time in the
        country.

MARY    Ah. (*He stares at her, intrigued despite himself.*)
        Is anything wrong?

BILL    Wrong?

MARY    I gather you have some sort of crisis on.

BILL    Yes.

MARY    Business, political or personal?

BILL    Look, do I know you?

MARY    The name's Mary Stewart.

| | |
|---|---|
| BILL | George told me. |
| MARY | He's very protective. Is he your paid heavy? |
| BILL | He's the hall porter — it's his job to be protective. |
| MARY | Does the name mean anything? |
| BILL | Should it? |
| MARY | I just wondered. May I sit down? |
| BILL | Not until you've told me why you're here. |
| MARY | Oh. (*She hesitates.*) |
| BILL | You seem nervous. |
| MARY | Well, this is a little difficult. (*She looks at a small painting of an impressionist landscape.*) Beautiful. Is that a Monet? |
| BILL | You haven't come to look at my paintings, I trust, young woman. |
| MARY | Oh, I like that. |
| BILL | What? |
| MARY | Young woman. Are you being flattering or patronising? |
| BILL | How old are you? |
| MARY | Not so very much younger than you. |
| BILL | You don't know how old I am. |
| MARY | Forty one. |
| | (*A beat.*) |
| BILL | Who the hell are you? |
| MARY | Let's say I'm someone with a genuine interest in your ... progress. |
| BILL | That could mean anything. News hack, private detective, business spy. Which is it? |

| | |
|---|---|
| MARY | I'm not playing hard to get, Mr Crayshaw. I'm just trying to take advantage of my . . . |
| BILL | Your what? |
| MARY | Anonymity — while I can. |
| BILL | Look, this is not the time for games. Tell me who you are, or get out. |
| MARY | Can't you guess? |
| BILL | Don't say a reporter. |
| MARY | It took you a long time. |
| BILL | Jesus Christ! You've got a nerve. Which rag? |
| MARY | Freelance, actually. But I sometimes cover political stories for the Sussex Chronicle. |
| BILL | You won't cover them much longer if I have anything to do with it. There are rules about these things and I know the Chronicle's editor very well. |
| MARY | It was he who suggested I came. |
| BILL | I don't believe you. |
| MARY | Why not? |
| BILL | His taste was never that good. (*She smiles.*) Besides we have an understanding. I let him have everything at the same time as the nationals, and he doesn't pester me except in an emergency. |
| MARY | Presumably he considers this an emergency. |
| BILL | What? |
| MARY | The death of your party agent. |
| | (*Pause.*) |
| BILL | You know about that? How? The body wasn't officially identified until a couple of hours ago. |

| | |
|---|---|
| MARY | (*shrugging*) I don't know how they found out. I only got the message to try and get to interview you about it. |
| BILL | Then why didn't you come through the normal channels? |
| MARY | Would you have agreed through the normal channels? |
| BILL | No. |
| MARY | Well, then. |

(*He hesitates, attracted and annoyed at the same time.*)

| | |
|---|---|
| BILL | All right, so what do you want? I can't tell you anything about it. I've only just found out myself. |
| MARY | How? |
| BILL | The police rang. A few minutes ago. |
| MARY | Why did they take so long? I gather it happened yesterday. |
| BILL | I was away. In any case the body was in such a ... they've only just properly identified it. |
| MARY | I'm sorry. No wonder you seemed distracted. |
| BILL | Yes. |
| MARY | Was he very valuable to you? |
| BILL | He's been my agent since I entered Parliament. |
| MARY | And from all accounts he handled a lot of your constituency work. |
| BILL | Agents do. What do you mean? |
| MARY | Just that you're perhaps even busier than most MPs. You must find that your time is very stretched. |
| BILL | Stretched? |

| | |
|---|---|
| MARY | You have this large financial empire. You travel to Europe and Asia on business. You're an MP. It's asking rather a lot isn't it? |
| BILL | I don't need much sleep. |
| MARY | So I heard. |
| BILL | (*choosing to ignore this*) And I have a very good back-up staff. |
| MARY | Such as Mark Tilling. |
| BILL | Yes. |
| MARY | So how will you manage without him? |
| BILL | I'll have to find someone else. Now look, I've only just recovered from the shock of hearing about it, so . . . |
| MARY | Well, actually . . . |
| BILL | What? |
| MARY | I had hoped to take advantage of this opportunity. |
| BILL | What opportunity? |
| MARY | To find out a little more. |
| BILL | About what? |
| MARY | You. |
| BILL | Meaning? |
| MARY | You see, I've been wanting to meet you for some time. I'm not just after a quick sensational news piece. I'm after something more . . . |
| BILL | Yes? |
| MARY | Meaningful. Of deeper significance. |
| BILL | Significance? |

| | |
|---|---|
| MARY | I'm interested in people who have access to power. I'd like to know what makes you tick, what your methods and your scruples are . . . if you have any. |
| BILL | Are you implying I haven't? |
| MARY | I'm not implying anything. I just want to find out. You should be flattered. (*She stops by a shelf of photos, notices one.*) Ah, the race-track. That must be you in your racing car days. |
| BILL | Yes. |
| MARY | Expensive hobby, that. |
| BILL | Come and see me tomorrow, Miss Stewart. |
| MARY | It'll be too late then. |
| BILL | Too late? |
| MARY | The story will have broken. Besides . . . |
| BILL | What? |
| MARY | The circumstances might not be so . . . . conducive. |
| BILL | I should have thrown you out right at the start. |
| MARY | Why didn't you? |
| BILL | (*after a moment*) Because you're an attractive woman, I suppose. Had you been male, or fat and fifty, you wouldn't have got past the door. |
| MARY | (*smiling*) Yes, I'd heard of your reputation. |
| BILL | And you were banking on that? |
| MARY | I wouldn't be so bold. (*She takes a pocket cassette recorder from her briefcase.*) Do you mind if I record this? Just for accuracy's sake. |
| BILL | Yes, I bloody well do! I haven't said I'm going to talk to you yet. |

| | |
|---|---|
| MARY | You can destroy the tape if there's anything on it you don't approve of — I promise. |
| BILL | Since when could one trust a journalist's promise? |
| MARY | Oh, come now. You're a big strong man. What's to stop you taking it from me and physically throwing me out? |
| BILL | Yes — that would make quite a story, wouldn't it? MP gets violent with pretty reporter. |
| MARY | I have been thrown out of places before. It's a professional hazard. |
| BILL | I think you should leave now, and save me the trouble. |
| MARY | Why? Have you something to hide? |
| BILL | Of course not. |
| MARY | Then what's the problem? |
| BILL | The problem is that it's eight o'clock at night, I've just received a very nasty piece of news, and I've got a lot of things to do because of it. |
| MARY | It's not just that you were going somewhere else? |
| BILL | Somewhere else? |
| MARY | I just wondered. |
| BILL | Where? |
| MARY | I don't know. Out to dinner, someone to see. I don't imagine you lead a cloistered life here in London. |
| BILL | How I spend my evenings is my own affair. |
| MARY | True. Then the sooner we get this over, the sooner I'll leave you to get on with your affairs. |

| | |
|---|---|
| BILL | (*amused, despite himself*) You're hard to believe. But you make a change from most of the arseholes who work in the media. |
| MARY | I hope that's meant as a compliment. |
| BILL | Perhaps they do things differently up in Edinburgh, or wherever it is you come from. |
| MARY | Aberdeen, actually. |
| BILL | Look, Miss Stewart . . . |
| MARY | Please call me Mary. |
| BILL | Press intrusion of privacy is a hot topic. Most of your readers would sympathise with me if I threw you out. |
| MARY | Actually, you wouldn't find it all that easy. |
| BILL | What do you mean? |
| MARY | I take judo classes to keep fit. They're the in-thing. |
| BILL | (*laughing*) Who's threatening who now? |
| | (*She takes a small automatic out of her handbag.*) |
| MARY | (*pointing it at him.*) I also carry this with me. |
| BILL | (*recoiling*) Good God! |
| MARY | (*smiling*) Don't worry — it's only a starting pistol. (*Returning it to her bag.*) Quite useful for deterring rapists, though. |
| BILL | Do you meet many rapists? |
| MARY | There are such people about, you know. |
| BILL | I'm well aware of that. |
| MARY | (*looking at a nude painting*) That's erotic. |
| BILL | Modigliani. I don't think he was a rapist. |
| MARY | (*inspecting a nude sculpture*) You like women's bodies, don't you? (*He says nothing. She looks enquiringly at him.*) |

| | |
|---|---|
| BILL | Men do. |
| MARY | Do you believe in evil? |
| BILL | Evil? |
| MARY | Genuine evil. As an elemental force in the universe. |
| BILL | What has that to do with women's bodies? |
| MARY | Nothing — necessarily. |
| BILL | Ah — it's the first of your 'in-depth' questions? |

(*She switches on the recorder.*)

| | |
|---|---|
| MARY | If you like. |
| BILL | No, I don't think I do believe in evil. |
| MARY | You don't? |
| BILL | There are reasons for everything. |
| MARY | Even the most apparently unjust of tragedies. |
| BILL | Yes. |
| MARY | So you would say that the purely fortuitous accident which happened to your agent, for instance, was part of some grand design. |
| BILL | I didn't say that. I said there must have been a reason. |
| MARY | Such as? |
| BILL | I don't know exactly what happened. |
| MARY | He was apparently driving on a perfectly wide, straight road. No other vehicle was involved. It was quite early in the morning so it's unlikely he was drunk. |
| BILL | Then he must have been careless, or there was a malfunction of the car, which meant it hadn't been serviced properly. These things don't happen for no reason. |

| | |
|---|---|
| MARY | No. I wonder — do you think I might have a drink? |
| BILL | I have to admire your gall. |
| MARY | As you noticed, I am a bit nervous. It took more courage than you know to talk my way in here. |
| BILL | Some honesty at last. (*He goes to pour her a drink.*) Whiskey, gin? |
| MARY | Vodka, please. As you're having. |
| BILL | How do you know it isn't gin? |
| MARY | You don't drink gin. |
| | (*He hesitates, lets that one go, and pours her a vodka and tonic. She wanders, looking at his art pieces, stopping and inspecting a Rodin piece about a foot high.*) |
| MARY | The Thinker. Is this an original edition? |
| BILL | Yes. One of fourteen or so. |
| MARY | (*whistling*) What's that worth? |
| BILL | Quite a lot. |
| | (*She picks it up.*) |
| MARY | Heavy. |
| BILL | Be careful with it, please. |
| | (*She replaces it and takes her drink from him.*) |
| MARY | Which is your favourite piece? |
| BILL | Of all of them? |
| MARY | Yes. |
| BILL | Why? |
| MARY | I wanted to know whether you collected them for their beauty, or simply as an investment. |

BILL        Cynical beast, aren't you? (BILL *points at a*
            *vase on a shelf near the fire-place*.) That Chinese
            vase, I think.

MARY        Why.

BILL        It's Ch'Ing dynasty porcelain. The first really
            good thing I ever bought. I love the colours,
            the texture.

MARY        You've done very well in business, haven't
            you?

BILL        It's taken a lot of work.

MARY        And a bit of help along the way.

BILL        What do you mean?

MARY        (*innocently*) Oh, just that having Lord Cargill
            for a father-in-law can't have exactly held you
            back.

BILL        (*amused*) Is provocation your sole interview
            technique?

MARY        It wasn't meant to be provocative. It was just
            a comment.

BILL        Yes, Lord Cargill has been very helpful to
            me. And I trust I have not abused his faith in
            me.

MARY        You haven't had any repercussions from that
            painful business of your first marriage then?

BILL        Repercussions?

MARY        Well it was awkward at the time, wasn't it?
            I've been looking at the cuttings. The press
            weren't very kind.

BILL        You can understand why I'm wary of them
            then.

MARY        You must admit, it did look a bit ... well,
            opportunistic.

BILL        Why?

| | |
|---|---|
| MARY | You'd only been married three years, I gather. And wasn't your wife pregnant with your first child? |
| BILL | These things happen. It was a mistake. |
| MARY | The marriage, or the child? |
| BILL | Both. I didn't feel good about it, I can tell you. |
| MARY | You looked very happy though — in the photographs of your second wedding. Quite a catch, Lord Cargill's daughter. |
| BILL | Yes, she was. |
| MARY | Certainly when compared to your first wife — Cara, was it? Unusual name. She was just an ordinary solicitor's daughter. |
| BILL | Her status had nothing to do with it. |
| MARY | Just a bad match. |
| BILL | Yes. |
| MARY | It must have cost you a bit though, the split. |
| BILL | I thought this was going to be an in-depth interview. It's beginning to smell more like a piece of tabloid prying. |
| MARY | I'm sorry. But what I'm trying to get at is, what makes a successful entrepreneur? How ruthless does one have to be? |
| BILL | I'm a legitimate businessman, not an entrepreneur. |
| MARY | Now perhaps. But it's taken you a while to get here. How much has it cost, I wonder? How much does one have to compromise in one's private life, one's ideals? |
| BILL | Not at all. |
| MARY | At all? |

BILL        One employs the same ideals in business as in the home.

MARY        That's what I meant.

BILL        Listen, Miss Stewart, you have very winning ways, but I'm getting increasingly uncomfortable about your tone. Have you any straight questions to ask?

MARY        Yes. What made you go into politics?

BILL        I'm interested in getting things done. What makes anyone go into politics?

MARY        All sorts of reasons. Power, influence, prestige.

BILL        More cynicism. It doesn't suit attractive women.

MARY        Why do you call it cynicism?

BILL        Isn't it?

MARY        Those are all things that women find attractive in men.

            (*A beat, filled with sexual tension.*)

            Can I ask another cynical question?

BILL        Well?

MARY        How did you manage to get the nomination for your constituency?

BILL        The nomination?

MARY        A political candidate is normally chosen on the basis of his past record.

BILL        So?

MARY        His work on behalf of the party. His participation in current affairs and so on. All rather dull stuff for a man like you. Yet none of the other candidates got a look in.

BILL        Perhaps I had other things to offer.

| | |
|---|---|
| MARY | Yes. Didn't your local party Chairman have financial problems around that time? |
| BILL | Sir Harry Turner? I wouldn't know. |
| MARY | It was fairly common knowledge that his company was in difficulties. |
| BILL | His affairs had nothing to do with me. |
| MARY | It's odd though, that shortly after your nomination they seemed to take a sudden turn for the better. Also that the Vice Chairman bought himself a very expensive new boat which he now keeps on the Hamble. |
| BILL | (*dangerous*) What are you saying? |
| MARY | I'm saying that I find naked ambition intriguing. |
| BILL· | (*after a moment*) You've only just heard about the accident. How have you had time to find out all this? |
| MARY | I told you, I've been wanting to write about you for some time. This just gave me the opportunity. |
| | (*He goes to the cassette recorder and switches it off. Takes out the tape and pockets it.*) |
| BILL | An opportunity I'd rather set limits to. |
| MARY | I didn't expect you to go along with that. It's not important to me. |
| BILL | What is important to you? |
| MARY | (*close to him*) Finding out what's important to you. |
| BILL | One of the hazards of being a politician is that you're vulnerable to unscrupulous hacks. Especially female hacks with blue eyes and prominent busts, who'll do anything if it gets them a good story. |

MARY            Stories aren't everything. There are some
                things I won't do unless I want to.

                (*Pause. They stare at each other.*)

                Tell me about Crayshaw Securities.

BILL            You're changing the subject.

MARY            No, I'm not. Naked success is
                very ... seductive.

BILL            Is it?

MARY            How did you found the company? Through
                your father-in-law?

BILL            It was founded under Lord Cargill's banner.
                Cargill Trust owns a large number of the
                shares.

MARY            That must prove frustrating at times.

BILL            Why?

MARY            To be constantly beholden to your own
                father-in-law. Never your own master.

BILL            He's been a very good master. We've always
                got on extremely well.

MARY            Do you get on as well with his daughter?

                (*Another pause.*)

BILL            My God, you push your luck.

MARY            I'm only querying the rumours.

BILL            You should know better than to believe
                gossip column prattle.

MARY            (*turning away and picking up another photograph*)
                Is this her? Pretty woman. You have a
                pension for blonde women, don't you?

BILL            It depends what they want from me.

MARY            Was your first wife — Cara — blonde?

BILL            No. Dark.

| | |
|---|---|
| MARY | (*replacing the photo*) What I'm saying is — presuming the rumours were true, and relations between you and your wife were not as happy as they might be — then having your career so at the mercy of her father must be rather ... inhibiting. Particularly when he's a Catholic, who doesn't believe in divorce. |

(*Pause. He says nothing. She comes close again.*)

Well?

| | |
|---|---|
| BILL | Where is this leading? |
| MARY | Wherever you choose to lead it. |
| BILL | Are you trying to entice me into bed, or into giving away something I might regret? |
| MARY | I imagine you very rarely give away anything you regret, Mr Crayshaw — or may I call you Bill? |
| BILL | Correct, I don't. |
| MARY | Then let's not rush things. (*Moving towards the office area.*) Do you do a lot of your business from here? |
| BILL | Some. |
| MARY | Is that a shredding machine? Why do you need that? |
| BILL | It's the best way to dispose of things you wish to keep from prying eyes. |
| MARY | Yes — it must come in useful. It's the talk of the City at the moment that you're planning a take-over of Cargill Trust. The offspring turning the tables on its parent. |
| BILL | So? |
| MARY | More ambition. |
| BILL | I need to expand. Make the step to the next dimension. What more logical than to take over the business to which I'm so closely tied? |

MARY        Yes. I imagine a man like you doesn't like
            being tied. Either to a wife who no longer
            attracts you, or to a father-in-law who might
            constrain you.

BILL        (*shaking his head*) You're a charmer, aren't
            you?

MARY        But rather a dangerous step, isn't it, the slave
            attempting to usurp the empire? Spartacus
            tried that, and look what happened to him.

BILL        Perhaps I'm better informed than Spartacus.

MARY        And you would do battle to the death with
            your own father-in-law?

BILL        He loves a battle. That's what he's in business
            for.

MARY        Even if it meant his own eclipse?

BILL        He'll emerge a hugely wealthy man. He's
            near retirement age in any case. What better
            end to a career than to hand over the reigns
            to your own son-in-law?

MARY        Leaving your own daughter's marriage in
            danger?

BILL        I never said that.

MARY        But is it true?

BILL        No, it is not. And what is more it's a highly
            presumptuous suggestion.

MARY        I apologise. Just testing the ground. (*A beat.*)
            I still . . .

BILL        Well?

MARY        Big business is fascinating. I still don't
            understand how a company can take over its
            own parent, which is several times its size.

BILL        Read the financial pages. They're following it
            all very closely.

| | |
|---|---|
| MARY | Oh, I do. I understand the theory of rights issues, and junk bonds, and raising capital from banks and so on. But in the end it all boils down to winning people over, isn't that right? In the end you have to persuade those whose favours you want to . . . to get into bed with you, to use a phrase. |
| BILL | (*coming close to her*) If the offer is attractive enough anyone can be seduced by anyone. |
| MARY | Can they? |
| BILL | You're well aware of that. |
| MARY | Yes. |
| | (*It looks as if he is about to kiss her.*) |
| BILL | The art comes in knowing how much is at risk. And at this moment I'm not risking anything. (*He breaks away.*) I think it's time you left. |
| MARY | (*her face changing*) Just as it was beginning to get interesting. |
| BILL | Yes. Pity. |
| MARY | From attraction to rejection so suddenly? |
| BILL | That's often the way it is with seductive offers. Now will you leave, please. |
| | (*She wanders towards where the Ch'Ing vase stands.*) |
| MARY | (*suddenly cold*) What do you have to offer though, Bill? That's what I'm interested in. |
| BILL | To whom? |
| MARY | To anyone. To Lord Cargill's daughter, who must have had the pick of the bunch. To the selectors in your constituency. To the supporters of your takeover bid. What is it you in particular have to offer that always seems to get you what you want? |

BILL            (*after a moment*) I've told you you're time is
                up.

                (*He advances on her. She casually picks up the
                Ch'Ing vase from its shelf and pretends to examine
                it. He halts.*)

                Be careful — that's very valuable.

MARY            You haven't answered.

BILL            Who are you? You're no journalist.

MARY            Why do you say that?

BILL            You don't talk like a journalist. You don't
                look like a journalist.

MARY            How do journalists talk and look?

BILL            Like people who want to stay in one piece.

MARY            You're bullying again. What is this worth?

BILL            More than you could ever afford.

MARY            I expect so. Is it insured?

BILL            That's neither here nor there. It's
                irreplaceable.

MARY            Ah. Would you mind giving me another
                drink?

BILL            Yes, I would. You were leaving.

MARY            I've decided not to — just yet. There are still
                some things to discuss.

BILL            Listen, lady. I don't know who you are, or
                what you're after, but I'm not the sort of man
                you can play these games with.

MARY            No. I'm sure you're not.

BILL            Try and get clever with me and you'll find I
                can play very rough.

MARY            Is that what Mark Tilling found out?

                (*Pause.*)

You look taken aback, Bill.

BILL    Mark Tilling? Is that where you got all this filth?

MARY    Why — did he know about it too? (*Pause.*) Bit of a slip, that. Rather given yourself away there, haven't you?

BILL    Who the bloody hell are you?

MARY    The question is, who are *you*? Are you an honourable man? Do you play according to the rules, or are you someone whose confidence can mean a stab in the back at any moment?

(*He starts towards her. She instantly raises the vase.*)

Don't come any nearer.

(*He stops.*)

BILL    You're on the wrong track. I'm not the villain you appear to think.

MARY    The evidence would not appear to support you.

BILL    What evidence?

MARY    The evidence Mark Tilling found, for one.

BILL    I thought so. You've been talking to him.

MARY    I can't talk to him any more though, can I? He's dead. Smashed up and burned to a cinder in his car. How convenient for you.

BILL    That was nothing to do with me. I was miles away, on my way to Frankfurt.

MARY    You weren't miles away the day before yesterday.

BILL    What the hell are you suggesting?

MARY    I'm asking whether you'll go to any lengths to get what you want. I'm asking whether you'll commit murder.

(*He starts for her with his fist raised. She calmly
lets the vase fall. It smashes in the hearth. Stunned
pause. He staggers back.*)

BILL    Jesus Christ! You're insane!

MARY    I don't think so. It's only a vase. What's that
against a man's life?

BILL    That was worth hundreds of thousands!

MARY    But you have millions more. (*Picks up 'The
Thinker'.*) There must be half a million's
worth here.

BILL    (*frightened now*) Don't! Don't please!

MARY    Oh, I imagine it would be hard to damage
this. Bronze, isn't it? It's very heavy. (*Replaces
it and moves towards the bookshelves.*) Fine
collection of old books too, I see. (*Takes one
down.*) Pilgrim's Progress. Very appropriate.

BILL    And very fragile — it's a first edition.

MARY    'I saw there was a way to hell, even from the
gates of heaven.' Wasn't that John Bunyan?

BILL    What do you want?

MARY    Just the truth.

BILL    What is your connection with Mark Tilling?

MARY    None. He's dead.

BILL    What was your connection?

MARY    I was hoping to marry him.

(*Long pause.*)

BILL    I see. (*Pause.*) I'm very sorry.

MARY    Are you?

BILL    I didn't know he was engaged.

MARY    You didn't know much about him at all.
Apart from his business capabilities. Do you
know much about any of the people who
work for you?

| | |
|---|---|
| BILL | I knew he had a girlfriend somewhere. Believe me, I had nothing to do with his death. |
| MARY | I'm not sure I do believe you. He was driving a new car, still under warranty. The police say it swerved off the road for no apparent reason. |
| BILL | It could have been anything. A dog, another vehicle. |
| MARY | There was a witness. Nothing like that happened. |
| BILL | These things *do* happen. Why do you suspect I had anything to do with it? |
| MARY | You are the only person who had a motive. |
| BILL | Motive? |
| MARY | Mark had found out about certain ... unorthodox activities connected with your take-over bid. |
| BILL | Is that what he told you? |
| MARY | As I think he told you. |
| BILL | He told me nothing. |
| MARY | I don't believe you. |

(*She goes to her briefcase and takes some sheets of paper.*)

I have his notes here. Details of various financial agreements and transactions. Photocopies of relevant certificates and bank-statements. Highly compromising evidence I would say.

| | |
|---|---|
| BILL | (*after a moment, in a low dangerous voice*) Where did he get those? |
| MARY | I think you know where. He told you all about them. |

BILL          (*holding out a hand*) Let me see them.

MARY          (*putting them back in the briefcase*) You're
              familiar enough with them.

              (*He strides to her and attempts to grab the case.
              With a sudden pull on his arm and a twist of her
              body she sends him sprawling on the carpet.*)

              I warned you I took judo classes.

BILL          (*sitting up on the floor*) I won't make that
              mistake again.

MARY          No, you probably won't. (*Picks up 'The
              Thinker' again.*) So I'd better see that you can't
              take me by surprise. (*She casually drops the
              statue on his foot. He yells in pain and falls back,
              clutching his ankle.*)

BILL          Christ Almighty! You've broken my ankle!

MARY          Oh, probably just dented it.

              (*He writhes in pain for a moment, then crawls to
              the sofa against which he sprawls, nursing his
              foot.*)

BILL          You maniac!

MARY          (*picking up 'The Thinker' and examining it*) It's
              all right, it's not damaged. (*She puts it back in
              its original place, and then helps herself to more
              vodka.*) Now perhaps you realise that I mean
              business.

BILL          What do you want?

MARY          Revenge.

              (*Pause.*)

BILL          What do you mean — revenge?

MARY          Just that.

BILL          On pure supposition that I've caused the
              death of your boyfriend?

MARY          It's much more than supposition.

| | |
|---|---|
| BILL | You've got evidence? |
| MARY | Let's say I know how it was done. |
| BILL | How? |
| MARY | Some intricate tinkering with the braking system, and a similarly sophisticated adjustment to the fuel injection, which caused the car to go up in flames after it crashed. Only someone who knows a lot about cars could have performed those operations. Someone who had been in motor racing, for instance. |
| BILL | (*still nursing his foot*) That's absurd. |
| MARY | Of course it would all have to happen when the car was travelling at high speed — on a motorway for example — so as to ensure maximum destruction. And in time, naturally. |
| BILL | In time? |
| MARY | To prevent Mark getting anywhere important with his evidence. Such as the Department of Trade and Industry? I believe he had an appointment with them in London yesterday. |
| BILL | The D.T.I.? |
| MARY | This sort of specialised crime is usually handled by them, isn't it? And I gather they're already quite interested in your affairs. |
| BILL | They're interested in anyone who handles major corporate transactions. I'm on very good terms with them, actually. |
| MARY | Do you bribe them, too? |
| | (*He has pulled himself up onto the sofa. She holds out her hand.*) |
| | May I have my tape back, please? |

| | |
|---|---|
| BILL | No, you may not. |
| MARY | Why? If you're innocent you have nothing to fear from a tape-recording. |

*(He hesitates, then takes it from his pocket.)*

| | |
|---|---|
| BILL | Very well, here it is. |
| MARY | Throw it to me. |
| BILL | Come and get it. |
| MARY | I'm not that foolish. Throw it please. |
| BILL | No. |

*(She takes the pistol from her bag and points it.)*

| | |
|---|---|
| MARY | Please. |
| BILL | *(laughing)* You can't scare me with a starting pistol. |
| MARY | I lied. It's a real one. |
| BILL | That piddling thing. I don't believe you. |

*(She pulls the trigger. There is a loud bang and an ornament behind his head shatters.)*

Bloody hell!

| | |
|---|---|
| MARY | The tape, please. |
| BILL | You wouldn't shoot me! |
| MARY | *(aiming the gun low)* Only your other ankle. To start with. |

*(He throws the cassette onto the floor. She picks it up, inserts it in the recorder and presses the record button.)*

| | |
|---|---|
| BILL | You are mad. You're unbalanced. |
| MARY | Possibly I am. To lose the person you love most in the world does unbalance one a little, I think. |
| BILL | What did you mean by revenge? |

| | |
|---|---|
| MARY | I intend to destroy your existence. As you've destroyed so many other people's. |
| BILL | How? |
| MARY | Piece by piece. |
| BILL | (*after a moment*) Look, I'm desperately sorry about Mark, I really am. But I had nothing to do with it, you must believe me. I'm in line for a junior minister's post soon. I wouldn't risk my entire career for the sake of some shady financial operations. |
| MARY | It's hard to stop the ball once it's rolling though, isn't it? How do you call a halt, that's the question? Do you say, all right, enough is enough — I won't go any further. Or do you, like Macbeth, go in deeper, ever deeper? Perhaps genuine evil is something that feeds on itself. An ever-expanding organism. |
| BILL | And you've decided I'm evil? |
| MARY | I don't know. That's what I want to find out. |
| BILL | How? |
| | (*She faces him, still holding the gun.*) |
| MARY | I'm going to put you to the test. |
| BILL | You sound like an Inquisitor. Are you packing a thumb-screw in that commodious bag? |
| MARY | I won't need anything like that. (*Casually indicating the service door.*) Where does that door lead? |
| BILL | The service stairs. I should have thrown you down them at the start. |
| | (*She wanders close to his collection of miniatures.*) |
| MARY | Are these porcelain? |
| BILL | (*apprehensive*) Meissen — eighteenth century miniatures. |

(*She picks up a miniature, and examines it.*)

| | |
|---|---|
| MARY | Pretty. What's this worth? |
| BILL | Don't — please. |
| MARY | Well, that depends on your answers. (*Smiles sweetly.*) Let's start with your first marriage. How old were you when you married your solicitor's daughter? |
| BILL | I don't have to go along with this. |
| MARY | (*holding up the miniature*) The Inquisition assumed silence to be a plea of guilty. |
| BILL | (*exasperated*) For God's sake . . . ! |
| MARY | It's a perfectly innocuous question to start with. How old were you? |
| BILL | Twenty eight. |
| MARY | And you loved each other when you got married? |
| BILL | Of course. |
| MARY | Yet the marriage only lasted three years. Did love turn to hate in so short a time? |
| BILL | Not hate, no. |
| MARY | No, she was after all pregnant when you left her. What happened to the child? |
| BILL | It died. |
| MARY | Died? |
| BILL | Before it was born. |
| MARY | Why? |
| BILL | There were complications. She had some sort of breakdown. |
| MARY | A breakdown? |
| BILL | Yes. |
| MARY | Over your parting? |

| | |
|---|---|
| BILL | (*angrily*) Over many things! |
| MARY | Did she still love you? |
| BILL | I don't know. The relationship had become impossible. |
| MARY | Impossible? |
| BILL | Yes. |
| MARY | Or merely inconvenient? |
| BILL | What do you mean? |
| MARY | By this time your work had brought you in with the big boys. The titans of the City. You were ambitious to join them. |
| BILL | So? |
| MARY | When you met Joanna Cargill — the daughter of one of the most titanic of them all — it must have seemed a gift from heaven. |
| BILL | Don't be so cynical. Joanna and I fell very much in love. |
| MARY | As you had done with your first wife, Cara. |
| BILL | I was more mature by then. I knew what I wanted. |
| MARY | What you wanted being to emulate Lord Cargill and build empires. |
| BILL | What I wanted being Joanna! |
| | (*She wanders as she speaks, still holding the miniature.*) |
| MARY | Let's move on a bit. Having married Joanna and established yourself in her father's business, you now begin to hanker after still broader horizons — such as politics. But how d'you gain a foot-hold there? How does a complete newcomer to politics manage to get support for his nomination? |

BILL        You tell me.

MARY        I suggest that you simply offered the right
            people lucrative tip-offs about your father-in-
            law's business operations.

BILL        What sort of tip-offs?

MARY        Oh ... advance information on company
            deals and take-over bids — I'm not up in that
            sort of thing. But of course in those days the
            rules about insider trading weren't so strictly
            enforced, were they? (*Pause.*) Well?

BILL        Quite untrue. (*She simply holds up the miniature
            over the hearth and lets it smash amongst the pieces
            of the Ch'Ing vase.*) For God's sake!

MARY        I warned you.

BILL        Are you going to smash something every
            time you get an answer you don't like?

MARY        (*picking up another miniature*) Every time I get
            an answer that isn't true. Well?

            (*She holds up the miniature. He hastily placates
            her.*)

BILL        All right, all right!

MARY        You admit it then?

BILL        I'll admit murdering my grandmother if it
            will stop you destroying everything I own.

MARY        We'll come to murder in a moment. So, in a
            remarkably short time, you were installed as
            MP for your local Sussex constituency. Where
            you also inherited a very bright and
            conscientious party agent called Mark Tilling.
            In fact Mark Tilling was so bright and
            conscientious that, in the course of his work
            for you, he uncovered these clues to the deals
            you had made with your selection committee.
            And, once his suspicions were aroused about
            those, they led inevitably to suspicions about

your business operations. (*She stops by the large picture window.*) What a glorious view. The whole of London at your feet. (*Turning back.*) By now you had begun to set your sights even higher in that field — on the entire financial kingdom of Lord Cargill himself.

BILL     One day I must employ you as my official biographer. You make my life sound so much more intriguing than it is. I need another drink.

MARY     By all means — help yourself.

BILL     I can't walk.

MARY     Oh, I'm sure you can.

(*She takes a furled umbrella from a stand in the lobby.*)

Here, have a prop. (*Tosses it to him.*) If you think I'm coming within your reach again, you're mistaken.

(*Using the umbrella as a stick, he limps across to the drinks.*)

BILL     Carry on. Which colourful chapter are we up to now?

MARY     The really interesting one, for followers of financial matters. How does a relatively minor operator such as yourself raise the cash to take over a vast business like Cargill Trust? Would you like to answer that? (*Waggles the miniature.*) And do be careful how you do so.

BILL     As a follower of financial matters you will know that you don't need to raise all the cash yourself. You can get other people who support the bid to buy shares. You can offer some of your own shares in exchange.

MARY     But they would be unlikely to join such a risky bid unless the rewards, and the guarantees, were pretty good. How do you

|  |  |
|---|---|
| | guarantee profits in a speculative situation like this one, Bill? Do you use straight bribes? |
| BILL | What can I say? I'd like that miniature to remain in one piece. |
| MARY | Terrible thing to be so controlled by one's own possessions. Let me answer for you. Mark found evidence of secret deals you've made with various firms and individuals in advance of their block purchases of shares in both Cargill Trust and your own company. Deals which I believe are variously known in the jargon as 'share-support' operations, 'success fee payments', 'buy-back guarantees' and so forth. All of which, are of course strictly against the law. |
| BILL | Therefore no one would be foolish enough to leave such evidence lying around. |
| MARY | Probably not. |
| BILL | So where would Mark obtain it — presuming it existed? He doesn't have the run of my files. |
| MARY | Inside information perhaps? |
| BILL | I would never let anyone on my staff know where such items were kept. |
| MARY | (*indicating her briefcase*) Well this stuff must have come from somewhere. It wasn't dreamed up out of the sky. |
| BILL | I haven't seen it yet. How do I know it isn't just sheets of rubbish? |

(*She takes the sheets from the briefcase again, and reads from them.*)

|  |  |
|---|---|
| MARY | 21st March. Charles Cawsley. Two million shares. Guaranteed b.b. — which I presume stands for 'buy-back' — price, 360p. 14th April. Martin Cook of Sheppard International. One million in Cargill Trust. |

|         | £500,000 s.f. — presumably standing for 'success fee', or some such. 19th April. R Goldberg, New York ... Need I go on? |
|---------|---|
| BILL    | Those could be records of anything. They prove nothing. |
| MARY    | Possibly not on their own. But I'm sure they would interest the inspectors of the D.T.I. At any rate enough to start them on a full-scale enquiry. Remember the Guinness scandal? |
| BILL    | They wouldn't find anything incriminating. I have nothing to be ashamed of. |
| MARY    | (*fiercely*) In which case, why kill Mark? |
| BILL    | I didn't. I'm not capable of murder. |
| MARY    | Even when everything you have is threatened? Your company, your fortune, your seat in the House of Commons — everything. |
| BILL    | No. |
| MARY    | I don't believe you. |
| BILL    | Then we must agree to differ. You can hardly put such a thing to the test. |
| MARY    | (*quietly*) Oh yes, I can. |
|         | (*Pause.*) |
| BILL    | I don't understand any of this. Perhaps you are truly mad. |
| MARY    | And what is madness? Merely something that so-called normal people cannot understand? |
| BILL    | Perhaps. |
| MARY    | Then certainly one of us is mad. |
|         | (*There is a pause as he stares at her curiously*.) |
| BILL    | How long have you known him? |
| MARY    | Mark? A year, almost to the day. |

| BILL | How is it that you and I have never met? |
|------|------------------------------------------|
| MARY | I keep very much out of his professional life. I have one of my own. |
| BILL | What is your profession? You're not a journalist. |
| MARY | I'm a lawyer. Useful in Inquisitions. |
| BILL | What sort of a lawyer? |
| MARY | Nothing too threatening. I work for a firm of solicitors in Sussex — probably too small for you to have noticed. |
| BILL | And you were going to marry Mark? |
| MARY | Yes. He had wanted to for some time. I was wary of such a commitment, but in the end I . . . |
| BILL | What? |
| MARY | I realised I was perhaps more capable of love than I had imagined — and so I consented. But all that is now gone. |
| BILL | I really am sorry. |
| MARY | I wish I could believe you. |
| BILL | How could I have tampered with his car? When would I have had the opportunity? |
| MARY | When you were down in the constituency two days ago. Mark came to see you at home there. |
| BILL | A routine meeting. He frequently came to my home when we had things to discuss. |
| MARY | Your wife was there also. |
| BILL | Joanna? Yes. |
| MARY | While Mark was there she heard you arguing in the study. |
| BILL | Have you been talking to her? |

| | |
|---|---|
| MARY | Yes. |
| BILL | When? |
| MARY | Yesterday. |
| BILL | What have you been saying to her? |
| MARY | Ah — has that got you worried? |
| BILL | She never mentioned it. I was speaking to her myself just before you arrived. |
| MARY | Perhaps she didn't wish to mention it. |
| BILL | Did you talk to her before or after you knew about the crash? |
| MARY | After. |
| BILL | You surely haven't burdened her with these wild accusations? |
| MARY | Nothing she didn't already suspect. |
| | (*Pause. They face each other, she calm, he bemused.*) |
| BILL | Very well, she heard Mark and I arguing. We frequently argued over constituency matters. It meant nothing. |
| MARY | You weren't arguing over constituency matters. You were arguing over the information he had collected. |
| BILL | What makes you think that? |
| MARY | I knew he was going to confront you with it that evening. And to tell you that unless you had an honest explanation, he had no choice but to go to the D.T.I. with it. I suggest that is when you made your mind up. |
| BILL | To murder him? |
| MARY | Mark was in some ways a rather naive person — he always believed the best of people. He wanted to give you the chance to justify yourself. |

BILL        I did.

MARY        No, you didn't. He came back to me that
            night a very unhappy man.

BILL        (*after a beat*) Have you any more revelations
            for me?

MARY        Such as?

BILL        I don't know. You've been conferring with
            everyone around me. Is there anyone else?
            Lord Cargill perhaps?

MARY        Oh, he will no doubt learn soon enough.

BILL        So in fact only you and Mark and my wife
            knew about all this?

MARY        That's right. And wives cannot testify against
            husbands. So now that Mark is out of the way
            you've only me to worry about. (*Pause.*) What
            are you going to do about that, Bill?

            (*The mobile telephone rings. She is nearest.*)

            I'll get it for you.

            (*She picks it up before he can get to it, putting the
            gun down on the desk at the same time.*)

            Hello? Who is this? Susie? Ah, I'm Mary.

            (*Listens for a moment, then turns to* BILL, *and
            speaks loudly for the telephone's benefit.*)

            Bill darling, it's someone called Susie who
            wants to know what's happened to you.

BILL        I . . .

MARY        (*cutting him off*) Would that by any chance be
            the bimbo you swore to me you were never
            going to see again? (*To the telephone.*) I'm
            sorry, he's been rather delayed. I suggest you
            don't hold dinner for him. You might be a
            long time waiting.

            (*Switches off the phone, and beams at him.*)

Talk your way out of that one.

BILL    You cow!

MARY    Tch, tch — very unparliamentary language.

BILL    Are you trying to destroy everything in my life?

MARY    Only the bits that aren't worth preserving. Though that doesn't appear to leave much. You don't seem to have a leg to stand on — if you'll pardon the joke.

BILL    (*holding out his glass*) Please fill my glass again.

MARY    Haven't you had enough to drink?

BILL    I need it.

MARY    (*turning away*) You managed quite well before.

(*He rises and once again limps to the drinks using the umbrella. He fills his glass, and then turns back, this time taking a closer line to the desk. She realises the danger, and starts for it too. As she reaches for the gun, he bangs the umbrella down on the desk, forcing her to jump back. He picks up the gun with his free hand.*)

BILL    Careless.

(*Pause. They face each other, he holding the gun, she the miniature.*)

Put down that miniature, please.

(*She looks at the miniature.*)

MARY    It's too nice to smash anyway. (*Puts it down.*)

BILL    Give me the papers.

MARY    (*calm*) What will you do? Shoot me?

BILL    If I have to.

MARY    Surely not. That really would be the end of everything.

BILL       Not necessarily.

MARY       Oh, come now. A body burnt to cinders in a
           crashed car is one thing. A body with a bullet
           in it, inside your own apartment is quite
           another.

BILL       There are ways round that too.

MARY       Now it's you who are fantasising. The police
           would have a field day. And the newspapers.

BILL       I'll worry about that. The papers, please.

           (*She casually picks up her glass and has a drink.
           He watches her cautiously.*)

MARY       So, the chips are down. No pretence any
           longer. You admit it all.

BILL       I admit nothing.

MARY       Then why such desperate measures to obtain
           a few second-hand pieces of paper?

BILL       It's a very critical time for the bid. Even the
           hint of a story like that could sabotage the
           whole enterprise.

MARY       Shooting me certainly would.

BILL       I've been working on this take-over for two
           years. I'm not going to see it fail now, just
           because you and your sanctimonious
           boyfriend come across a few irrelevant
           transactions!

MARY       Irrelevant transactions. A good phrase for
           corruption on a grand scale.

BILL       Those sort of deals go on all the time.
           They're what makes the commercial wheels
           go round. It's the way of the world, you
           foolish woman!

MARY       So you admit it all?

BILL       (*fiercely*) Yes! Make what you can of it.

| | |
|---|---|
| MARY | (*quietly*) Thank you, I will. (*She goes calmly to the cassette recorder, switches it off, and puts it in her briefcase.*) |
| BILL | You don't think you're going to walk out with that, do you? |
| MARY | Bill, like most bullies, you're all bluster when it comes to a face-to-face contest. Killing a man by remote control, is one thing. But shooting someone in cold blood in your own drawing-room is quite another. Besides which, even you aren't clever enough to think of a story which would explain that to the police. |
| BILL | Don't take the risk. |
| MARY | Why not? I have nothing more to lose — unlike you. |
| | (*She starts to walk towards the lobby.*) |
| BILL | Don't. I'm warning you. |
| | (*She stops at the threshold of the lobby and turns.*) |
| MARY | Pure evil. Does it exist? Now we'll find out, won't we? |
| | (*She turns towards the front door. He fires. She staggers, and turns, clutching her shoulder. He fires again. She clutches her stomach with both hands, and sways for a moment, staring at him. She lifts one hand from her stomach and stares at it. It is covered with blood. She looks back wide-eyed at* BILL, *then collapses on the floor and lies motionless.*) |
| BILL | Oh, God! |
| | CURTAIN |

## ACT TWO

*A few seconds later.*

BILL *stands with the gun in his hand.* MARY *lies on the floor where she has fallen.*

BILL          Oh, my God.

              (*He limps across and looks down at her. Kneels
              beside her and puts his ear close to her mouth.
              Rises and stands for a moment in thought. Pockets
              the gun. Using his handkerchief to avoid
              fingerprints, he picks up her briefcase from where it
              has fallen, opens it and takes out the cassette
              recorder. He extracts the tape and pockets it.
              Returns the recorder to the case. Takes out the
              sheets of paper and pockets those. Carefully wipes
              all surfaces clean of fingerprints with the
              handkerchief. Leaves the case beside the body. Goes
              to the house phone and taps a couple of numbers.*)

              George? Is the cellar store-room unlocked? I
              need to collect something from it. Thanks.
              And is Arthur still on duty in the basement
              car park? Could you call him for me and ask
              him to bring the Rolls round to the lift
              entrance? I'm transferring some books to a
              dealer friend of mine and I have to load
              them into the boot. No, I can manage,
              thanks.

              (*He replaces the receiver, and goes to the fireplace
              where the shattered pieces of china lie. Picks up a
              piece, looks at it, tosses it back in the hearth. Goes
              to the front door, opens it, has a last glance at the
              inert form, then switches out the lights and leaves,
              closing the door. The lift is heard descending.*)

              (*A few moments of silence. Then the body stirs,
              moves, and rises. She switches the lights back on,
              and surveys the room. Takes off her spectacles (if
              they haven't already fallen off in the fall), picks up
              her handbag, takes it to the desk, and sits behind it.*

*First, she wipes the 'blood' from her hand with a
tissue. Then with some haste takes out various
make-up articles and erects a small mirror on the
desk. She holds open each eye in turn and extracts
coloured contact lenses, which she puts away in a
small case, then strips off a blonde wig to reveal
dark hair underneath which she brushes out into a
very different style from the wig. She carefully peels
off false eyelashes and wipes the shading from her
eyes, eyebrows and cheeks with cream, and does the
same with her lipstick. She then applies some more
subtle shading to her features, and redraws her
eyebrows.)*

[NB: *Much of the subtler changes of make-up —
contact lenses, eyelashes, eyebrows — can be
mimed, as long as they convince the audience.*]

*(Lastly, she reaches inside her shirt and extracts
padding from her bra. She is revealed as a petite
brunette of quite different aspect. She looks down at
her considerably reduced bust measurement and
sighs briefly. Puts her accoutrements away in the
bag. Stands and scans the various paintings on the
walls. Goes to the Monet, and lifts it down from its
hook. Takes it to the desk and, with the aid of a
steel paper knife, extracts the painting from its
frame. Takes the painting to the shredding machine
and places it in the shredding slot. Picks up her
drink and goes to switch out the lights again. The
sound of the lift rising is heard. She hurries across
the room in the half-darkness, and sits in a chair
facing the lobby.)*

*(A key is heard in the lock and the front door
opens.* BILL *enters backwards, dragging a trunk
behind him. Heaves it into the room and switches
on the lights. Sees her, and stands dumb-founded.)*

CARA    *(in a normal English accent)* Hello, Bill.

BILL    Cara. What ... *(Looks at where the body had
been.)* Where ... ?

CARA    Didn't know I was such a good actress, did
you?

BILL        Good God!

CARA        There were a few moments when I thought
            you'd guessed, but it seems I got away with it.

BILL        (*dazed*) I don't understand. What ... ?

CARA        What was it all for? I told you, revenge.

BILL        Revenge? For what? That was all over ages
            ago. We haven't seen each other for years.

CARA        I've seen you.

BILL        Where?

CARA        Oh, in the papers, on television. And on
            occasion in the flesh. I know you've hardly
            given a thought to my existence since you left
            me, but I've been very aware of yours.

BILL        (*taking the gun from his pocket*) The gun ... ?

CARA        Blanks. Only the first bullet was real.

BILL        You planned the whole thing?

CARA        I couldn't plan the end result. I didn't know
            how you would react.

BILL        Then what ... ?

CARA        As I said, Bill, I wanted to discover just how
            genuinely evil you were. You rose to the
            challenge magnificently.

            (*Pause. He is still bewildered.*)

BILL        But Mark. All that stuff about Mark, and
            his ...

CARA        Collected evidence? That was all true.

BILL        You mean, you and Mark Tilling were ...

CARA        Lovers — yes. And planning to marry.

BILL        I still don't understand.

CARA        Sit down, Bill. Take the weight off your poor
            ankle.

            (*He sits opposite her.*)

|        | I must say you look good after all this time. The strain hasn't taken its toll. |
|--------|---------------------------------------------------------------------------------|
| BILL   | Strain?                                                                          |
| CARA   | (*gesturing round the room*) Of acquiring all this. Come a long way, haven't you — since we were struggling newlyweds? I always knew you'd make it. I don't expect I've worn so well. You knew about my break-down? |
| BILL   | Yes.                                                                             |
| CARA   | It was a long time ago now, of course. But these things have a way of staying with you. |
| BILL   | Cara . . .                                                                       |
| CARA   | I do want you to understand why all this is happening, Bill. I'd hate you to feel at the end that you were the victim of injustice. |
| BILL   | What was that . . . charade all in aid of?                                       |
| CARA   | I had to be sure. I had to know whether you really were capable of murder as well as all the other things. |
| BILL   | And now?                                                                         |
| CARA   | I can finish the job. I can wreck your life as you've wrecked mine.              |
| BILL   | Surely the fun and games are over?                                              |
| CARA   | Oh no, Bill. I haven't started. After all you've done to me that was just a taster. You see, people like you have to be made responsible for their actions. Otherwise you think you can go on forever trampling over others. Well now you're going to find out what it's like to be trampled on. |
| BILL   | You've got me wrong, Cara. You always did.                                       |
| CARA   | Did I? Well, let's go back over things and see if you can convince me. Only this time there will be a price to pay if you don't. |

| | |
|---|---|
| BILL | Price? |
| CARA | For every piece of someone's life which you've destroyed, I will destroy a piece of yours. Tit for tat. That's fair, isn't it? But first I need some life insurance for myself. |
| BILL | What do you mean? |
| CARA | You've proved you'll go to any lengths — even murder to stop me. It took me a while to work out how to protect myself. After all I can only smash so many Meissen figures. But I think I have the solution. (*She rises and looks around the room.*) I never credited you with such sophisticated taste. You have some lovely things. |
| BILL | There aren't many left intact. |
| CARA | (*smiling*) You do love your art collection, don't you? Far more than people really. |
| BILL | It's certainly more stable. |
| CARA | But just as destructible. Look around, Bill. Do you notice anything missing? |
| | (*He scans the room.*) |
| BILL | The Monet. You bitch — you've taken the Monet! |
| CARA | I wasn't sure which would be your favourite piece now that the Ch'Ing vase has gone. But I reckoned that was probably the most valuable. |
| BILL | Where is it? |
| CARA | Here. (*She goes to the shredding machine, and switches it on. A light glows.*) I can understand why you need a shredding machine. Gets rid of all sorts of unwanted stuff, doesn't it? Whole volumes chewed into nothing at the press of a button. |
| BILL | You couldn't. Even you couldn't do that. |

CARA   I could if you threaten me. So just remember
       — I can move a lot quicker than you, and if
       you try anything, it only requires me to reach
       this button for Monet's beautiful cornfield to
       end up as shredded wheat.

       (*From this moment she stays between him and the
       shredding machine.*)

       Now ... the next step. This is where your fax
       machine comes into the game. So clever of
       you to provide all these modern amenities.

       (*She switches on the fax machine, and opens her
       briefcase.*)

BILL   What are you going to do with that?

CARA   (*taking some sheets from her briefcase*)
       Despite ... or perhaps because of all that's
       happened, no one yet knows about your
       various exploits. No one except you and I.
       Neither the D.T.I. nor the police have
       anything definite to go on — except perhaps
       their own suspicions. I have here three
       sheets, especially prepared for the fax
       machine.

       (*Separates the sheets.*)

       One for the Chairman of the Tory Party —
       listing the details of all those remarkably
       lucky share dealings pulled off by your local
       selectors. One for the D.T.I. — setting out
       the various financial shenanigans connected
       with the Cargill take-over bid. And lastly, one
       for the police, describing the circumstances of
       Mark's bizarre car accident.

       (*Hands him three more sheets.*)

       Here — I've thoughtfully provided you with
       copies.

BILL   (*glancing at the sheets*) You've been working
       hard at all this, haven't you?

CARA    Where one's life is at stake it doesn't do to leave things to chance. Now ... wonderful inventions these, aren't they? Instant communication at any time of the night or day.

BILL    (*dry*) A mixed blessing, apparently.

CARA    Yes. Well let's start at the beginning, and see if you can provide reasons to stop me sending any of these.

BILL    I doubt if you're receptive to any sort of reason at this stage, Cara.

CARA    Oh, as a lawyer — yes, that part was true — I'm always receptive to genuine reason. Right, are you comfortable? Let's begin. How old was I when you left me, Bill? Do you remember?

BILL    Twenty two, or three.

CARA    Twenty three, and seven months pregnant.

BILL    So?

CARA    I was stunned that you could just walk out on me like that. I was in a daze for months — I didn't know who I was, or what I was doing. And then — women's bodies being what they are — the trauma of it all caused me to lose the baby. After that I didn't care whether I lived or died.

        (*She picks up the photo of his wife.*)

        I knew from local gossip that you had taken up with Joanna Cargill, and I read all about the wedding, yet I still could not accept that you had simply abandoned me after all we'd ... It just didn't seem human.

        (*Replaces the photo.*)

        What is your explanation?

BILL    I gave you my explanation at the time. Frequently, and at great length.

| CARA | I didn't accept it then, and I don't now. That you had genuinely fallen out of love with me at such short notice, and equally in love with her? After all I can still turn you on, can't I, Bill? I proved that earlier. |
|------|------|
| BILL | Yes — you must have got quite a kick out of that. |
| CARA | Quite fun seducing your ex-husband incognito. But of course I couldn't offer what she offered. Such a quick route to the top of Lord Cargill's business empire. |
| BILL | Cara, we went through everything ad nauseam all those years ago. I'm not going to resurrect the same dreary arguments again now. |
| CARA | Not even to explain why you never even made contact afterwards? You paid me my allowance regularly, but never made the slightest attempt to find out what had happened to me — or the baby. Incredibly callous behaviour, wouldn't you say? |

*(He says nothing. She goes to the fax machine.)*

Well then, it looks as if you've failed the first test.

*(Selects one of the sheets in her hand, and places it in the machine.)*

We'll start with the message to your Chairman at Conservative Party Office.

| BILL | Cara ... |
|------|------|

*(He starts to rise. She puts her finger on the button of the shredding machine.)*

| CARA | Careful, Bill. |
|------|------|

*(He sits again. She taps in a number on the fax machine.)*

Anything to say?

| | |
|---|---|
| BILL | Nothing I haven't said already. |
| | (*She presses the transmit button. The sheet slides through the machine.*) |
| CARA | That one is for the baby I lost — a political career in exchange for a life. Now — your business career. Mark was quite clever in finding out about that, wasn't he? |
| BILL | How did you get to know Mark? |
| CARA | We met quite by accident, believe it or not. When I found out who he was I suppose I saw him as a means of getting closer to you. |
| BILL | Ah. |
| CARA | Till I began to love him for his own sake. |
| BILL | Why did neither of you tell me? |
| CARA | Oh, it wouldn't have done his career any good if it got out that he was consorting with your first wife. |
| BILL | (*grim*) No. |
| CARA | But that was nothing to his dilemma when he discovered the tricks you'd turned over your selection. And your even more devious manoeuvres over the Cargill take-over. |
| BILL | I'm intrigued. I do wish you'd tell me what he thought he'd found. |
| CARA | It's quite useful having an ex-wife on your side, Bill. She can come up with all sorts of inside information. |
| BILL | Such as? |
| CARA | Oh . . . your working methods, your daily routine, how you keep your personal records. You see, with my help it was a simple matter for Mark to search your files for evidence. |
| BILL | Which files? |
| | (*She gestures at the filing cabinets.*) |

| | |
|---|---|
| CARA | These files. |
| BILL | He got into the apartment? |
| CARA | I remembered how you always left your keys in your left hand coat pocket. When we were married I had to darn the holes in several. |
| BILL | So you did. |
| CARA | Mark simply had to borrow them when you left your coat hanging in the constituency office, and have duplicates made. |
| BILL | How did he get past George? |
| CARA | (*indicating the down-stage door*) He used the service stairs. However he didn't find quite enough here to incriminate you. There are some records you can't risk keeping even amongst your personal files, aren't there? Records that are so sensitive you actually have to keep them constantly on your person. |
| BILL | You mean like in spy movies? Microfilms shoved into orifices? |
| CARA | No, just your little notebook. In which you list the details of every private agreement you ever made, and every company you secretly dealt with. |
| BILL | Ah. |
| CARA | I think I was the only person you ever showed it to. You boasted you had enough information in it to take over a dozen businesses. In those days it was a tattered miniature diary full of pencil scribblings. I gather it's a much more elegant thing now — black leather and gold initials. |
| BILL | That's right. |
| CARA | But still small enough to fit into your spectacle case. You *are* paranoid about anyone seeing it, aren't you? Have you got it with you now? |

(*He reaches into his inside breast pocket and takes out his spectacle case. He extracts from it a small notebook.*)

Old habits die hard, don't they, Bill?

BILL     So Mark found his way into this, did he?

CARA     Do you remember losing your spectacles a week or so ago?

BILL     Yes, I do.

CARA     They went missing for almost twenty-four hours. You were in a great panic, Mark said. Highly relieved when they turned up behind a bookshelf in the constituency office.

BILL     And that little shit had them all the time.

CARA     Very revealing that little book proved. Once he had learned to decipher your personal shorthand.

BILL     A few scribbled notes on the sort of deals that are done every day in the City.

CARA     The sort of deals that have landed several eminent men in gaol over the years.

BILL     I could convince the authorities there's nothing illegal about them.

CARA     Can you convince me though, Bill? That's the point.

(*She goes back to the fax machine.*)

It's me you have to prove your innocence to.

BILL     For God's sake, Cara!

CARA     (*inserting the second sheet*) I'm waiting. I want a good reason why all those privately recorded agreements don't add up to criminal market rigging. Otherwise the D.T.I. can have them and make up their own minds.

BILL     How can I explain? It would take hours to go through all my various transactions!

| | |
|---|---|
| CARA | (*tapping in the number*) You have thirty seconds. |
| | (*He starts towards her. She puts a finger on both the fax transmission button and the shredder button.*) |
| | Which is it to be, Bill? The Monet or the D.T.I.? There's a dilemma — your business career or your finest picture? |
| | (*He gasps with frustration, and turns away. She presses the button on the fax machine, and transmits the message.*) |
| | That's that then. Your career for my marriage. Fair exchange, don't you think? |
| BILL | Insane, Cara! You're quite insane! |
| CARA | And finally we come to the big one. Mark. My second chance at love. |
| | (*She gestures at the fax machine.*) |
| | This was what he threatened you with, wasn't it? Exposure. And you had no alternative but to silence him before he could go to anyone. |
| | (*Pause.*) |
| | Well? |
| BILL | Look, Cara — I'm sorry if you ... I didn't know that you and he ... |
| CARA | Would that have made any difference? If you'd known about us, would that have stopped you doctoring his car? |
| BILL | Supposing it turns out it was doctored? What evidence have you it was me? |
| CARA | Who else could it have been? |
| BILL | Are you saying I was his only enemy in the world? |
| CARA | Possibly not. But you see ... |
| BILL | Yes? |

| | |
|---|---|
| CARA | He saw you. |
| BILL | Saw me? |
| CARA | Working on the car. |
| BILL | When? |
| CARA | He had an invitation to stay to supper the night he came to see you. You could hardly rescind it after your row. But over supper there was a distinctly tense atmosphere. I gather you hardly spoke a word throughout the meal. |
| BILL | Did my wife tell you that? |
| CARA | (*ignoring this*) She and Mark made polite conversation, and then, while they were having coffee, you excused yourself saying you had some business calls to make. Mark presumed you were phoning fellow conspirators to warn them of his exposure. However, some ten minutes later he excused himself to go to the toilet. |
| BILL | Go on. |
| CARA | Didn't foresee that, did you? The window of your downstairs toilet looks out over the garage fore-court at the side of the house. Mark noticed a moving light outside the window, peered out, and saw you with a torch doing something to the dashboard. He couldn't make out what you were up to, though. |
| BILL | I told him what I was up to. |
| CARA | Yes. When he confronted you about it. You said you were searching the car for the photocopies he'd made of your papers. Good excuse — he believed you, since they were actually in the boot of the car at the time. |
| BILL | Ah. |

| | |
|---|---|
| CARA | I believed it too — until after the accident. Then I put two and two together. |
| BILL | (*after a moment, with a slow nod*) I see. |
| CARA | That's all down here on the fax to the police. Have you anything to add before I send it? |
| BILL | (*wandering towards the lobby*) It's all still speculation. None of it is genuine evidence. |
| CARA | It will be enough to initiate a proper forensic examination on the car. Along with my evidence that should be sufficient. |
| BILL | What makes you think you'll be allowed to give your evidence? |
| CARA | How can you stop me? |
| BILL | I am between you and the door. |
| CARA | Oh, Bill . . . |
| BILL | And you haven't a gun to wave at me now. |
| CARA | Surely you're not going to try and get rid of me again? Having made such a hash of it last time. |
| BILL | What have I got to lose? You've sprung all your surprises now. And I know about your judo, and your pistols, and your clever disguises. What have you left? |
| CARA | The Monet. |
| BILL | Ah, but when it's between that and my own safety, then there's no choice. |
| CARA | I'm warning you, Bill — try anything and I'll press the button. |
| BILL | Well before you do, I'd like to show you something. |
| CARA | What? |
| | (*He has moved into the lobby and reaches up to the wall.*) |

BILL            My fuse box.

                (*Before she realises what he is doing he has opened
                the lid of the fuse box and switches off the
                electricity. All the lights, as well as the fax machine
                and the shredder, go off.* CARA *gives an
                exclamation. The room is in darkness except for the
                faint glow of the city through the window.*)

                Now what, Cara?

                (*Pause. She backs away from him in the half
                darkness.*)

CARA            Don't let's make this a squalid little chase
                round the furniture.

BILL            I can wait my chance.

CARA            You don't understand though, Bill.

BILL            What?

CARA            I don't actually care what happens to me.

BILL            What do you mean?

CARA            I have nothing left now — except the
                satisfaction of tormenting you a little before
                the finish.

                (*They have circled each other in the darkness, and
                she is now near the lobby. She makes a dash for the
                front door and manages to get it open before he
                reaches her. In the light from the passage he is seen
                to grab her round the waist and lift her back into
                the room. She elbows him in the stomach,
                temporarily winding him, and escapes back inside
                the room. He manages to shut the front door,
                closing off the light from the passage again.*)

CARA            (*from the darkness*) Nearly had me then, Bill.
                Tell me — how were you planning to leave
                your second wife?

BILL            Leave her?

| | |
|---|---|
| CARA | Were you going to abandon her? Wait until the take-over was completed, and then just walk out as you did on me? |
| BILL | What makes you think I want to leave her? |
| CARA | Oh come, Bill — you're not going to tell me you love her. What about all the girlfriends? |
| BILL | Gutter press garbage. |
| CARA | And is Susie on the telephone just gutter press garbage? |
| BILL | Susie is none of your business. |
| CARA | Wrong, Bill. Everything you do is my business. |

(*She is doing something in the darkness.*)

| | |
|---|---|
| BILL | What are you doing now? |
| CARA | I'm bringing this little game to an end. |

(*He switches on the lights again from the fuse box. She is revealed as having picked up the mobile phone.*)

Thank you, that's better. It's hard to dial in the dark.

(*He holds up an automatic pistol and points it at her.*)

| | |
|---|---|
| BILL | Stop. |
| CARA | (*doing so*) Ah. |
| BILL | That's enough. The fun is over. |
| CARA | (*nervously*) Where did that come from? |
| BILL | I keep it in the fuse box. One little hiding place you weren't able to tell your boyfriend about. |
| CARA | No. |
| BILL | We MPs lead precarious lives these days — there are so many nut cases around. Put the phone down, please. (*She hesitates.*) Put it down! |

(*She does so.*)

Who were you phoning?

CARA   The police.

(*He raises the gun as if to fire. She backs away, frightened.*)

Now what? Are you going to make it a double killing?

(*He doesn't answer, merely aims the gun more deliberately.*)

This one wouldn't be as easy to explain as the car crash.

BILL   Oh, yes. A plea of self-defence. Very credible since you came armed yourself, and your gun has been fired all over the apartment. Are you afraid now, Cara? How does it feel to have *your* life threatened?

CARA   Even you aren't clever enough to explain away two deaths at once, Bill.

BILL   Mark's death had nothing to do with me.

(*He goes to the fax machine and takes out the sheet, then puts it in his pocket.*)

And now I won't even have to explain it.

CARA   I think you will.

BILL   Why?

CARA   I'll show you.

(*She opens the door to the service stairs. The body of a man, hideously defaced with blood and burns, its clothes singed and tattered, swings out, suspended by a loop of rope from a hook on the back of the door. BILL recoils with a gasp of horror. The corpse hangs there for a moment, then she tugs at the rope and it falls on the floor at her feet.*)

|  | Just so you realise the consequences of what you have done. |
|---|---|
| BILL | How in heaven's name ... ? You're sick! |
| CARA | I'm not the one who's sick. (*She stifles her emotions.*) However I do feel a bit sick now. If you'll excuse me I'll use your bathroom. |

(*She goes out into the lobby. He stares for a long moment at the dreadful figure on the floor. Wipes his head distractedly. Makes up his mind. Goes to where the trunk stands, and opens the lid. Then returns to the body. Trying not to look at its features, he stands astride the corpse and bends down to drag it to the trunk.*)

(*At that moment the corpse sits up and grasps him round the throat.*)

(BILL *gives a terrified shout and straightens, holding the figure's wrists. For several seconds he wrestles with the apparition, choking, half throttled. He manages to get his hand into his jacket pocket and pulls out the gun. He fires it into the air. The loud report causes the figure to release him, and* BILL *falls back onto the floor, gasping and retching.*)

(*The figure runs out of the service door, and vanishes.* BILL *crawls to a chair and leans against it, gasping, for several seconds. then pulls himself up into the chair.* CARA *returns.*)

| CARA | (*calmly*) Oh, has he gone? |
|---|---|
| BILL | (*hardly able to speak*) You are crazy. Both of you. |
| CARA | I told you I hadn't finished with you, didn't I? |
| BILL | What a sick stunt. |
| CARA | Quite effective, I thought. |

(*He pulls himself together, goes to the drinks, and pours himself some soda water. Recovers his composure and turns to face her.*)

BILL        So. Mark wasn't killed?

CARA        No.

BILL        Then what was all this in aid of?

CARA        It was a miracle we weren't killed.

BILL        We?

CARA        I was with him in the car.

BILL        (*after a moment*) What happened?

CARA        We were on our way to London to the D.T.I. We were going quite fast on that long straight just before joining the M23. It was raining. We came up behind a lorry, which suddenly braked. Mark braked too, but for no apparent reason the brakes failed. He pulled the wheel hard over to the left. We left the road, rolled over several times down a bank, and ended miraculously the right way up in three feet of water. It was a stream, or a ditch, or something. It saved our lives. I was semi-conscious, caught up in my safety belt, but I was aware of an explosion and a blast of hot air. Then the front of the car was under water and the fire died. Otherwise we would both have ended up looking like that. (*She gestures toward the door.*) Bad luck for you — as it happened we were able to climb out relatively unscathed.

BILL        And you assumed I had tampered with the car?

CARA        That was when Mark remembered seeing you and your torch the night before.

BILL        So then between you, you thought up this melodrama?

| | |
|---|---|
| CARA | We just thought we'd get a little of our own back before turning you over to the police. Mark has gone to call them now. |
| BILL | Have you got them on your side too? |
| CARA | What? |
| BILL | The police phone calls. To me and to Joanna. Informing us of the crash. |
| CARA | (*smiling*) Oh, those were Mark. An extra little touch to add authenticity. Makes quite a good desk sergeant, doesn't he? |
| | (*He puts the gun in his jacket pocket and sits on the sofa.*) |
| BILL | My congratulations. You worked it all out very cleverly. |
| CARA | We had to. The only way we could prove anything was to get you to confess. Which you've now done. |
| BILL | I've confessed nothing. |
| CARA | I think the record will show that you have. |
| BILL | What record? |
| | (*She goes to the bookshelves, takes out a row of false book backs and reveals a built-in cassette recorder. A red light glows intermittently on and off.*) |
| CARA | This was something else Mark knew about. |
| BILL | Ah. |
| CARA | More paranoia. Do your opponents know you record everything they say in here, Bill? |
| BILL | Foolish of me to show him that. |
| CARA | I thought it might be wise to have a back-up to my own tape. As you can see this is recording now. |
| BILL | For how long? |

CARA          Since I had a look at your 'Pilgrim's
              Progress'. (*She switches it off and extracts the
              cassette*.) Except of course during your little
              power cut. (*The telephone rings. She answers it*.)
              Mark, darling, are you all right? Yes, I'm
              fine. Good — I'll tell him. (*She switches off the
              telephone*.) The police are on their way. He
              warned them I might be in danger. So, what
              are you going to do now?

BILL          (*shrugging*) Sit and wait for them to arrive, I
              suppose.

CARA          You're just going to wait for them to come
              here? Open up your whole can of worms?

BILL          I can't stop them now, can I? But I have
              nothing to fear. Only your word and some
              highly spurious evidence.

CARA          (*holding up the cassette*) I don't imagine they'll
              find this spurious.

BILL          What will that prove?

CARA          Quite a lot, I think. Now — I don't think I
              want to spend any more time with you.
              We've said all there is to say. I'll wait for the
              police downstairs in the lobby.

BILL          (*taking out the gun again*) I'd rather you
              stayed, please.

CARA          Oh come on, Bill — we're not going through
              that routine again?

              (*He goes to the front door. Takes some keys from
              his pocket and double locks the door from the
              inside*.)

BILL          We still have some unfinished business, Cara.

CARA          You don't have much time. And the police
              won't appreciate being locked out.

BILL          I'll let them in — when I'm ready for them.
              (*He crosses to the service door and locks that also*.)
              When I've finished with you.

| | |
|---|---|
| CARA | More threats? |
| BILL | You've declared war on me. Very well. Let's play it out to the end. |
| CARA | We're at the end, Bill. |
| BILL | Oh, no. I haven't had my turn. You like these games of intrigue and deceit. Let's play another. |
| CARA | (*apprehensive*) What game? |
| BILL | (*looking at his watch*) How long have we got, d'you think? Five minutes? And the police have been called about a possible murder, haven't they? |
| CARA | So? |
| BILL | So, why don't we give them one? |
| CARA | You wouldn't kill me with the police on their way? |
| BILL | Oh, but it wouldn't appear that *I* had killed you. |
| CARA | Who then? Who else is there? |
| BILL | Mark Tilling has been here all this while, hasn't he? Only just rushed out of the building. |
| CARA | You couldn't possibly pin it on him. He called them. |
| BILL | Couldn't I? Let's think this out logically. (*He works it out as he goes along.*) First of all the genuine facts. You are my first wife. We split up for reasons that no one could understand. They all thought it very strange that I should have abandoned you when we had such an apparently happy marriage, and you were seven months pregnant. Supposing that in fact it was all something cooked up between us? |

CARA        Cooked up?

BILL        Supposing we had agreed that, if I could, I
            should hook Joanna Cargill and take
            advantage of it to work my way up her
            father's business empire. Supposing the
            divorce had been for show — behind it you
            and I had a pact. In fact we secretly
            maintained our relationship, despite the
            tragic loss of our baby.

CARA        Highly improbable.

BILL        Not at all. (*He moves in close to her and caresses
            her hair from behind.*) You've proved you still
            know all the sexual tricks, haven't you, Cara?
            Got me quite worked up at first.

CARA        (*turning towards him*) Did I?

BILL        (*backing away again*) And of course I did
            continue to keep you in considerable
            comfort. In fact it was a very clever
            arrangement. Because of my career I had to
            spend much of my time away from home —
            with every opportunity of still seeing a lot of
            you. The problem arose when I went into
            politics. We used to use my agent, Mark
            Tilling, as a go-between. He was party to our
            secret liaison. But what we hadn't foreseen
            was that he would become infatuated with
            you himself. His desire for you made him
            unbalanced. He became obsessively jealous of
            my relationship with you. He actually went so
            far as to have keys made to my apartment so
            that he could spy on me. He made copies of
            all sorts of private business documents in the
            hope that he could destroy my reputation.
            Things came to a head when he came to my
            house the night before last, and I confronted
            him about his spying activities. We had a
            row, as Joanna will testify, and I demanded
            his resignation. Now the crash ... how did
            that happen? Yes — like this. One of his last

duties for me was to drive you down to London — en route to the House of Commons where he had some final business to clear up. Now it's well known that Mark was always a highly erratic driver. He's had several narrow squeaks in the past. On the way up from Sussex he lost control of the car, ended up in a ditch, and almost killed you both.

(*A police siren is heard in the distance.* BILL *stops to listen as it draws near, passes, and fades away again.*)

Not for you, I'm afraid. To continue — you were lucky. You recovered from the crash and made your way to London this evening, leaving Mark to sort out the car. That's when it all came to a head. Mark knew we had planned to meet here as soon as I got back from Frankfurt. He came here himself to confront us. He let himself in with his duplicate keys, and hid behind the service door. You meanwhile arrived in blonde wig and spectacles so that no one would recognise you — as George downstairs can testify.

(*He takes her gun from his pocket.*)

As we were sitting here, discussing how to deal with the situation, Mark jumped out and attempted to kill us both. He fired this gun, which he had taken from your handbag earlier. He and I struggled. I still have his finger marks on my neck. He was like a madman, hurling things about, smashing several of my most valuable pieces. He injured me — caught my foot — crippled me for several moments, which gave him time to turn his attention to you ... and shoot you with the gun. (*Indicating the gun.*) No, that's no good — only blank bullets left.

(*He places it on the coffee table. Indicates his own gun.*)

With my gun. No good either — no
fingerprints on it.)

(*Places that beside the other.*)

Got it!

(*He goes to where the rope lies on the floor, and
picks it up.*)

He strangled you with this rope. Much
better. The forensic people will probably find
all sorts of clues linking it to him. While he
was struggling with you, I recovered enough
to get my own gun. I fired it into the ceiling
which frightened him off. Too late to save
you however. He ran from the building and
rang the police before I could myself —
trying to frame me. Grief stricken, I cradle
your body as they arrive. How does that
sound?

CARA        You're not serious?

BILL        (*coming towards her with the rope*) We should
            get on with it before they get here.

CARA        (*backing away*) The fax messages. How do you
            explain those?

BILL        He sent them. To try and incriminate me.

CARA        (*desperately*) The tape recordings.

BILL        I'll wipe them as soon as I've finished with
            you.

            (*He has cornered her against a wall. She threatens
            him with a judo stance.*)

            Ah yes, I must watch out for the judo,
            mustn't I, Cara?

            (*They struggle. He smacks her hard across the face.
            She falls back and he loops the rope around her
            throat.*)

CARA        (*screaming in terror*) No!!

(*He tightens the rope around her neck, and she begins to choke. He holds her for several moments, and she sinks to her knees. Then at the last minute he relaxes the rope.*)

BILL     No, I've got a better idea.

(*He lifts her onto a chair. She collapses, gasping and shocked. He takes her arms behind the chair, and ties them with the rope.*)

Had you really frightened there, didn't I? I'm glad to see you *can* be frightened.

(*He stands back and surveys her.*)

How do you feel now?

CARA     What are you going to do?

BILL     Stop pretending for a start. Let's cut out the make believe, shall we? Let's speak the truth from now on — do you think that's possible?

CARA     What do you mean?

BILL     Do you know the meaning of the word truth, Cara?

CARA     Try me.

BILL     Very well. Firstly, the police aren't coming. Mark never called them, did he?

CARA     Of course he did. He was frightened for my safety.

BILL     No. They'd have been here minutes ago after a call like that. But it was all part of the masquerade, wasn't it? The police are the last people you two want to see.

CARA     Why?

BILL     Cara, Cara, I know you. I lived with you for three years.

CARA     So?

| | |
|---|---|
| BILL | I lived with your illusions and your fantasies and your neuroses. You were on the verge of insanity then, and you haven't changed. And Mark is almost as much a case as you are. You deserve each other. |
| CARA | Are you trying to make out we are the evil ones? |
| BILL | I don't believe in evil, as I told you. But I do believe in delusion. |
| CARA | Delusion? |
| BILL | From start to finish, my dear Cara. You never saw me in a true light — even at the beginning when we were so unrealistically in love with each other. |
| CARA | You admit that then? |
| BILL | Oh, yes. I was as infatuated with you as you were with me. I was charmed by your wayward imagination, your romantic eccentricities. But it wasn't long before I saw you in your true colours. And the more I became disillusioned the more you became paranoid. |
| CARA | Paranoid? |
| BILL | In public you remained all sweetness and light, but in private our life together was intolerable. You must admit it. |
| CARA | Only because of your infidelities. |
| BILL | Imagination, Cara. I wasn't that sort of man. But you had to see a blonde behind every door. Deception in my every move. And then of course you decided you wanted a baby. |
| CARA | Ah yes, the baby. |
| BILL | That was going to be the solution to all our problems. By then I knew it was the last thing I wanted, but you became obsessed about it. Manic! And so you tricked me into getting you pregnant. |

CARA          I did not!

BILL          Oh yes, Cara. You went off the pill without
              telling me, and one night after we'd been out
              to a dinner party you turned on all your
              feminine charms — which I might add you
              had denied me for some time — and you
              trapped me. Well that was the final straw.
              From then on I knew I had to get out.

CARA          Oh, so Joanna had nothing to do with it?

BILL          She would never have come between us if
              things had been right. But as it was she
              provided everything you could not. Stability,
              sanity, support . . .

CARA          Support all right!

BILL          (*angrily*) I mean mental support, not material.
              It was sheer coincidence she was Lord
              Cargill's daughter. It wouldn't have mattered
              if she'd been the daughter of his chauffeur.

CARA          Didn't do you any harm though, did it?

BILL          No, it didn't. I'm very grateful for all that
              Lord Cargill has done for me. But that was
              incidental. I was lucky. It wasn't a cunningly
              preplanned scheme as you persisted in
              believing.

CARA          Then why did you just abandon me? Why
              did you have nothing to do with me after you
              left?

BILL          You were dangerous, Cara! You followed me
              around, you sent threatening letters, you
              spread rumours to the media and to anyone
              else who would listen. You were deranged!
              And every tiny sign I gave that I wished to
              remain on amicable terms, you took as an
              indication that you could win me back. I
              didn't dare make contact. But I saw that you
              were well looked after financially. And,
              contrary to your belief, I kept an eye on your
              welfare.

CARA            Huh!

BILL            When you had your breakdown after losing
                the baby, who do you think arranged for you
                to go into that expensive clinic? Santa Claus?
                And then, when you finally pulled yourself
                more or less together and applied for a job in
                your solicitor's firm, it was I who dropped a
                word in the right ear to get it for you. Just a
                clerk, not a lawyer as you like to call yourself,
                but a secure niche nevertheless.

CARA            How thoughtful.

BILL            Then you met Mark Tilling. I didn't find out
                for quite some time. He's a secretive man in
                all sorts of ways, isn't he?

CARA            You knew about us?

BILL            Eventually.

CARA            How?

BILL            Joanna told me. Someone in the constituency
                whispered to her. You can't keep these things
                secret for long. I waited for Mark to tell me
                himself, but he never did. That's when I first
                began to mistrust him. No, not true — I'd
                had my suspicions for a while.

CARA            What suspicions?

BILL            Well, he never really approved of me as his
                MP from the start. Thought I'd come up the
                easy way, thanks to my family connections.

CARA            Hadn't you?

BILL            No, Cara, I hadn't. I had no easy options
                from Lord Cargill, I can tell you. I had to
                work my guts out. I had to prove myself
                every inch of the way.

CARA            You certainly proved yourself to the
                constituency committee.

BILL    Yes, I did. They didn't choose me because I
        bribed them. They chose me, I like to think,
        because they knew me well as a local man
        and thought I was right for the job.

CARA    The fact of their buying into Lord Cargill's
        businesses being quite incidental.

BILL    They were backing a man and an outfit they
        knew something about, and which they
        believed in. That's usually how sensible
        investments are made! But Mark wouldn't
        have that. Oh no, he had to see sculduggery
        at every turn. He sniffed around my affairs
        like a dog after dynamite! Is it any wonder I
        was neurotic about hiding records?

CARA    The Cargill Trust takeover. You can't deny
        all that.

BILL    Of course I don't. It's common knowledge!
        And, much to your disappointment, it's all
        being done with Lord Cargill's approval.

CARA    I don't believe you. Why would he agree
        to ... ?

BILL    He's seventy five years old, Cara! He wants to
        retire and enjoy some of the fruits of his
        efforts. And what better way than to sell out
        to his own son-in-law.

CARA    Then why all the deals?

BILL    It's an enormous operation! Half the
        predators in the City would like to beat me to
        it. I can't do it on my own. Of course I have
        private agreements with people! Of course I
        obtain promises of support, which I keep
        records about. It'll all come out in the open
        when the time is ripe — there's nothing
        illegal. But your boyfriend wouldn't have
        that, would he? In his warped mind it all had
        to be dirty insider dealings, and suspect
        share-support schemes.

CARA      You had them listed in your secret little book.
          Success fees, and guaranteed buy-back prices,
          and . . .

BILL      Imagination again, Cara. 'Guaranteed b.b.
          price' does not mean 'buy-back price'. It's my
          shorthand for 'bought below price' —
          meaning that the other party has guaranteed
          to buy a certain number of shares before they
          reach a certain price — at which point I can
          bank on having those shares on my side.
          'S.F.' does not stand for 'success fee' — it
          stands for 'slush fund'. The amount a
          company has agreed to put up towards the
          huge costs of the operation. And so on, and
          so on. All perfectly innocent, you see.

CARA      Clever explanations, but I don't believe you.

BILL      No, well I wouldn't expect you to. Nothing
          will cure you of your delusions, poor Cara. I
          learnt that long ago, when you were
          convinced that every time I came home
          twenty minutes late meant I was up to
          something suspicious. Every time I looked at
          another woman meant I was having a wild
          affair with her.

CARA      Does Joanna have the same delusions then?
          Does she have such false suspicions about
          Susie, for instance?

BILL      Not at all. She and Susie get on very well
          together.

CARA      What?

BILL      Susie is my personal secretary — Suzannah
          Jones. She's fifty years old, plain as a
          pumpkin, and very unbimbo-like. She's also
          an excellent cook, and frequently gives me
          supper at her flat when I've been away for
          a while, so that we can catch up on all my
          mail and other business. She no doubt found
          your conversation hilarious, and won't let me
          hear the end of it when I see her.

| | |
|---|---|
| CARA | There are others. I bet Joanna knows it as well as I do. |
| BILL | Despite our ups and downs, Joanna and I are very happy together. She is my greatest support — without her I could never have got where I am. (*He picks up a piece of china from the hearth.*) And incidentally it was she who chose that Ch'Ing vase you so wantonly smashed. |
| CARA | (*a hint of hysteria in her voice*) I don't believe you — I know you too well! You use people. You're using us! |
| BILL | Cara, calm down. |
| CARA | You'd make up any kind of story. You're evil! |
| BILL | Cara . . . |
| CARA | The car crash! What about the crash? |
| BILL | I don't know. If indeed you did have a crash — which I'm beginning to doubt — then I'd attribute it to Mark's driving. You said it was raining yesterday — I wouldn't be at all surprised if he wasn't driving extremely dangerously in the neurotic state he was in, and simply skidded out of control. And then, having survived it, the two of you thought — right, let's make use of it. Let's tie it all into the general fantasy and present it as a murder attempt by me. And my racing past, and my being seen searching his car for those papers the night before all fitted in nicely, didn't it? |
| CARA | But you have attempted murder. You did tonight! You can't deny it. I set you up with that gun and you tried to shoot me! |
| | (*He shakes his head, smiling.*) |
| BILL | No, Cara. I aimed well wide. When you 'died' so realistically I knew something very strange was up, so I went along with the pretence to see what would happen. |

| CARA | You knew? You knew I wasn't dead? |
| BILL | Oh yes. |
| CARA | You didn't know who I was? |
| BILL | I'm afraid I knew that, too. |
| CARA | How? |
| BILL | It was a long time ago, but we were after all married for three years. I began to get odd feelings about you early on. Clever disguise, but there was something about the way you moved, the way you phrased things. Then, when you mentioned your relationship with Mark Tilling, everything suddenly fell into place. I went back nine years, and the nightmare of that time was all about me again like a cloud. I wasn't far off aiming that gun straight at you, I must admit. However I didn't. |

*(Pause. She slumps in her chair, and starts weeping. He comes to her and unties the rope. Then he picks up her drink and hands it to her.)*

Come on, Cara. It was a good try, and you had great fun for awhile, but it's over now. Go home, and forget me. You and Mark can start an amateur dramatic society, or something.

*(The house intercom phone rings. BILL answers it.)*

Yes, George? Oh yes, I'm sorry. Tell Arthur, I won't be going out now after all — he can put the car away. And please apologise to him.

*(As he talks, CARA gets up behind him and goes to the coffee table where he has left the two guns. She picks up his, and points it at him. He turns.)*

*(after a moment)* How foolish of me to untie you.

| | |
|---|---|
| CARA | I'm so tired, Bill. I'm so sick of it all. Following you about all these years, trying to get close to you. I can't take any more. |
| BILL | What do you mean? You love Mark. |
| CARA | No. I've never loved anyone but you. I just wanted to have you back. I wanted to get you away from that bitch and her filthy-rich family. |
| BILL | (*indicating the fax machine*) You've spent the whole evening trying to destroy me. |
| CARA | Not really. I wasn't sending those faxes where I said I was. They went to your own constituency office. Mark will find them in the morning. |

(*He shakes his head ruefully.*)

But I can't go on any longer. If I can't have you, then no one is.

| | |
|---|---|
| BILL | Cara, come on now. You need help. Don't make it worse. |
| CARA | It's the perfect way, Bill. Quick and certain. How many bullets are there in here? One for each of us? That's all I need. |
| BILL | Can't you see that an obsession like yours is unreal? You need help to get better, Cara. I'll get it for you. |
| CARA | You can't do anything for me any more, Bill. You've made that quite clear. It's over now. |
| BILL | (*stepping towards her*) Cara … |

(*She pulls the trigger. There is a loud report. Nothing happens. He still stands there.*)

Sorry, that really is a starting pistol. No use to you, I'm afraid.

(*He goes to her and takes the gun gently from her. She sits again, weeping. He picks up her own gun,*

*and empties it of the blank bullets. Then takes her
handbag, and puts her gun into it. Hands her bag
and briefcase to her. She rises in a dream. He takes
her to the door, unlocks it with his keys, and ushers
her out.)*

Tell Mark he'd better have cleared out his
desk before I get back to Sussex. And you
stick to your own desk at the solicitors. They
tell me you're very good at your job.

*(He sees her to the lift, then returns, closing the
door behind him. The lift is heard descending. He
pours himself another drink. The telephone rings.
He answers it.)*

Hello? Yes, Geoffrey. Wonderful. And what
about New York? We're home and dry then.
Splendid — I'll break the news of our official
bid tomorrow. Now listen, Geoffrey — this is
important. Destroy any notes or records that
may be incriminating. *Everything*, you
understand. There mustn't be a whiff the
D.T.I. can latch onto. Someone's been
sniffing around at this end, and they got
damned near to scuppering us. I'll do the
same thing here. Fine.

*(Disconnects, then taps a number on the telephone.)*

Hello, Susie, my darling. Sorry about all that.
It was some nut case of a reporter. I'll
explain when I see you — I'll be there in ten
minutes. And be prepared to celebrate,
beautiful. We've won the takeover battle and
you and I are free. *(He grins.)* Good — don't
bother to get dressed again.

*(He switches off the phone, then puts the gun in a
drawer. Goes to the shredding machine and takes
out the Monet. Looks at if fondly for a moment,
then puts it carefully in a drawer. Takes the
various papers from his pocket, and shreds them in
the machine. Then takes the little notebook from his
spectacle case. Smiles ruefully, then shreds that*

*also. Takes a bottle of champagne from the drinks
cabinet, switches off the lights, and goes to the front
door. Opens it, and we see him silhouetted for a
second against the passage lights. A shot rings out.
He staggers and falls back into the room.* CARA
*appears in the passage, her gun in her hand, and
stands staring down at his body.)*

CURTAIN

# Properties List

*Office Area*

Desk, chair

TV Monitor

Fax Machine

Shredding Machine

Mobile Telephone

Intercom Telephone

Cassette Recorder (hidden behind books)

Gun (preset in fuse box)

Umbrella Stand (with umbrella)

Trunk (preset offstage)

Rope (body)

BILL:

Overcoat (keys in pocket)

Spectacle Case, containing:
  Spectacles
  Small notebook
  Handkerchief

*Living Area*

Sofa, armchair

Drinks Cabinet, containing:
  Vodka
  Tonic, Soda Siphon
  Ice, Glasses
  Bottle of Champagne

Sculptures (inc. 'The Thinker')

China Miniatures

Vase

Paintings on Wall (inc. 'Monet')

Photographs on Mantle

MARY/CARA:

Briefcase, containing:
  Assorted papers for faxing
  Pocket cassette recorder & tape

Handbag, containing:
  Automatic pistol
  Assorted cosmetics
  Spectacle case